# THE WORD EQUITY™ MODEL

## THE ESSENCE OF INTENTIONAL SPEECH THAT ADDS VALUE TO OTHERS

DOMINIQUE KENNEDY, MS, CCC-SLP

YVES PUBLISHING

ISBN: 978-1-7348653-4-9

# CONTENTS

# ABOUT THE AUTHOR

Dominique is the author of several published works. Dominique Kennedy is an experienced and licensed Speech-Language Pathologist. Dominique earned a bachelor's degree and master's degree in Communication Sciences and Disorders with an emphasis in Speech-Language Pathology. Her experience across settings includes schools, hospitals, rehabilitation centers, and early intervention agencies. Through her private practice, she serves children and adults. She is a certified member of the American Speech-Language-Hearing Association (ASHA) and has held memberships with Special Interest Groups (SIGs) Fluency & Fluency Disorders and Augmentative & Alternative Communication. Through her desire to empower individuals and families, she has developed educational programs, professional development courses, and workshops. Dominique lives in the Atlanta Metro area of Georgia with her husband and their two daughters. She enjoys fine arts, music, and culture.

Website: www.dominiquekennedy.com

# WORDS MATTER

Word is defined as
: distinct meaning in a particular field
: something that is said
: stated observation with regard to a common experience
: stated declaration to do/not do something

Equity is defined as
: the practice of giving to others what they're due
: the quality of being fair and impartial
:value; worth; valuation; ownership; rights; proprietorship

*The Word Equity™ Model is defined as the essence of intentional speech that adds value to others.*

# THE WORD EQUITY™ MODEL

## THE ESSENCE OF INTENTIONAL SPEECH THAT ADDS VALUE TO OTHERS

Word Equity™ Series

# WORD EQUITY™ MODEL
## STRATEGY SCREENER

What is the best way to apply a strategy to master my goal(s)? ...for better communication skills?

- For better outcomes personally?
- For better outcomes professionally?

What are the advantages of using this strategy?

▪ How does the strategy support my overall mission and vision: for connecting and nurturing? Toward clarity of the message conveyed?

▪ In what ways does this strategy improve my overall quality of life: alignment with values? For increased connections?

▪ How does my decision to use this strategy help my relationships: achieve a greater impact? Relationship longevity?

- Have I considered my needs and clearly communicated my expectations: participants needed for buy-in? Methods or skills I will need to apply?

- What's required: strategic planning? Support of family/friends/stakeholders?

- What are the other considerations for this strategy to be effective: trade-offs? Benefits?

- How can the goal be achieved: through resources or attributes that I possess? Through resources I can obtain?

- What is my desired time-frame for mastery: 3-week challenge? 3-month challenge?

- Have I clearly defined my purpose for using this strategy: expected outcomes? How will I know that the goal has been met?

DOMINIQUEKENNEDY

# WHEN YOU TRANSCRIBE IT, DID IT TRANSLATE?

I'll be the first to admit, I've butchered my fair share of songs, the most infamous line depicting my lyrical lapse found me belting out the words "back down in Zaberls," and I bet you can't guess which 90s hip-hop hit song that line is derived from. Before I tell you which song and the actual transcribed version of the lyric, let me just say in my defense I'd not fully developed the prefrontal cortex, which controls impulse (so instead of researching the lyrics, I just went with what sounded correct) nor had I developed the most optimal organizational skills in this area (so instead of restructuring the lyrical pattern in context I sloppily assigned an order of pseudowords and again went with what sounded correct). Read a book on neuroscience, and you'll also discover that the brain doesn't fully mature until age 25, which makes me wonder why western culture has deemed an 18-year-old as an adult and 21 years old as the legal age to consume alcoholic beverages. I digress. Back to my epic fail. So my poor attempt at lyrical prowess landed me at "back down in Zaberls" for the melody which actually reads "black diamonds and pearls" Mind you, "If I Ruled The World" by Nas, featuring Lauryn Hill was the grammy-nominated hit song for best rap solo performance in 1997, and I bet that I was the only one singing that part of the song completely wrong. To this day, I have a good laugh about that musical mishap. Now go on and look up the accurate lyrics of this song and while you're at it, check out the songs that you have on repeat and tell me if you are actually singing every line the way that the songwriter wrote it.

So what's my point? How often are we simply spewing words and thinking nothing of where they land and how? How often do we assign meaning to a thing in life without assessing it for its finite parts? It wasn't necessarily the first song in history that I personally "remixed," and it will not be the last. The difference now is that I'm more intentional about words and examining them for their true essence rather than just saying what seems to fit. Have you ever actually assessed how many ways this may show up for you in your life? Beyond song lyrics (guilty!). Beyond misquoting popular sayings and known proverbs (don't act like I'm the only one who likes a good proverb). Beyond mispronouncing a person's name (I know people who are notorious for this). How often do you take the time to listen to what was said by a communication partner, let alone consider what was said in response?

If I have not yet made this completely clear, I'm borderline obsessed with words as a communication science professional and author. I am a logophile, a self-proclaimed word nerd. I absolutely love words. For their multiplexed meanings, for the color and complexity that they add to a given statement. Wordplay and wit are friends and foes. So what happens when there are misfirings in the flow of

4

communication. What happens when we miss out on an opportunity to connect simply as a result of miscommunication. We must find ways to maintain the integrity of what we intend to communicate. I challenge you as a conversationalist to do a deep dive into the words you wield and examine what you are saying when you speak. When you make a statement, through words, you give guidance to what is spoken. Each word should serve its rightful purpose. Don't underrate the continuity of purpose in your message.

## MINDSET RESET

The Word Equity™ Model is more than just a "say this, not that" attempt. It is a full-on mindset reset. It is filtering thoughts through a valuation system with emphasis on distinctive qualities characteristic of a detectable expression. For some, implementation of the Word Equity™ framework will be a paradigm shift. For others, application of the Word Equity™ framework will further refine how you choose to show up in your established relationships. How one views the world and how one chooses to take up space is easily shaped by the thoughts we have and the words we speak about our ever-changing situations and life experiences. It seeks to promote authenticity and produces language that honors self and others. Through effective use of the Word Equity™ Model, one can better approach practical parenting, sustain harmonious households, reconcile and restore relationships, foster lasting friendships, and be well respected in the workplace.

# WORD EQUITY™ MODEL WORDPLAY

While it is not my goal to create clones, I am optimistic that we can each find ways for the Word Equity™ Model to show up in our daily lives as conversationalists. Due to the Word Equity™ Model, I am mindful of the ambience that words serve to supply a space either by casting light or inviting darkness. I believe that words spoken by me or those around me contribute to the maintenance or disruption of equilibrium.

An utterance in itself conveys a way of thinking. That which is shared by a communicator helps the listener gain insight into how he thinks, how he allows his feelings to show up, and perhaps why he says the things he says. While this may sound more like a character analysis, it is a method of carefully weighing an exchange's nature and considering how it may be interpreted. How we choose to connect and with whom is largely based on exchanging thoughts, ideas, perspectives, ideologies, often through the words we speak to one another. Sure we can assign infractions to the current climate, but what would you say of your state of affairs before what we'd like to deem as unprecedented times.

I have chosen to meticulously examine what I believe is at the core of what we must further employ: the foundational unit of a given exchange, the words we speak about a thing, and the language we use to tell about our lived experiences. Let us not neglect the fact that each experience counts.

I charge you to consider how you show up in conversations. Assess the very nature of how you present. Did you fully connect to the points made, or did you just switch subjects and move on? How often do you leave the conversation feeling that you were fully present and completely understood? Let's consider your strategy to clearly communicate during the future exchanges that you desire to have.

I'd like to provide some examples of how I've expressed myself through the Word Equity™ Model. (Remember that the Word Equity™ Model is defined as *the essence of intentional speech that adds value to others.*)

**A common response to a child-** *"Good job!"*

*Spoken through the lens of the* **Word Equity™ Model-** *I love the way you think. I noticed how focused you were on completing your work. You appeared to be very committed to the task that you selected. I can imagine the fulfillment that you get through expressing yourself in this manner.*

**A common response to a significant other-** *"You're amazing!"*

*Spoken through the lens of the* **Word Equity**™ **Model-** *You are a wonder. Quite an exquisite work of art. These words that you breathe out that dutifully take form and shape as directed by their source. How I love to behold them. I adore their brilliance. Eagerly I take them in for as long as these words that act as luminaries will allow. I study every curve, every shade, every arrangement, basking in it. Warmed and filled by it. Gazing out at the mirage of an image that they form, knowing it is you that I see in all your glory.*

**A common response to a disagreement-** "I'm over it!"

*Spoken through the lens of the* **Word Equity**™ **Model-** *I'd like the opportunity to be very open and honest with you. When you expressed your opinion about the topic that we were discussing, I'll admit that I didn't readily agree (in fact, I still don't); however, I'm willing to put forth the effort to understand things from your perspective.*

**A common response to a colleague-** "Okay, sounds great!"

*Spoken through the lens of the* **Word Equity**™ **Model-** *Thanks for sharing your thoughts on that, I'd be happy to consider what you've said.*

I foster an environment that reinforces the positive impact that words have on the human spirit.

— DOMINIQUE KENNEDY

# CONSERVATION THROUGH CONVERSATION

The Word Equity™ Model is accomplished by mindfully maintaining and carefully protecting a relationship's value through the words that are exchanged. It is allowing your words to reflect the esteem you intend to express toward your communication partner. By choosing your words carefully, a communicative exchange's integrity is deemed worthy of the honor placed on it. So instead of speaking recklessly, words are expressed respectfully.

Acknowledgment of the following principles contributes to adherence to this framework.

The principles are as follows:

What I present communicates.
What I present is meaningful.
What I present is valuable.
What I present has influence.

**Principle One: What I present communicates.**

When you connect with the notion that what I present communicates, you will also become more self-aware. Every part of our being communicates something. An eyebrow raised, wrinkling of the forehead, narrowing the eyes, the swiftness of a head tilt, posture, arms folded, hands-on-hips, or fingers locked. Yes, all of these gestures communicate a message. Even how you enter a room communicates. This is all done without even saying a single word.

**Principle Two: What I present is meaningful.**

As you connect with the notion that what I present is meaningful, you will become more mindful of the words that you choose to speak. There is significance in what you express. There is a purpose for every utterance that is released from your lips. Allowing yourself to believe that what you say is important and should be measured with care will better enable you to mindfully weigh the words that are exchanged with others and those spoken or unspoken about yourself.

**Principle Three: What I present is valuable.**

While you connect with the notion that what I present is valuable, you will more readily consider the usefulness of the communicated words. Taking the time to truly explore the impact and value placed on words will further determine the function served by what is stated. In turn, viewing your words as desirable or esteemed will challenge you as a communicator to choose words that appreciate and enhance rather than undervalue and reduce.

**Principle Four: What I present has influence.**

Once you connect with the notion that what I present has influence, you will examine your words' capacity to take shape or take root in the hearts and minds of others. You will assess the condition or development of the relationships you have established to determine if the words you exchange within a given relationship cause positive influence or whether it creates negative interference.

*It is important to weigh your words properly so the message is communicated appropriately, as this either adds value or devalues your communication partner.*

— DOMINIQUE KENNEDY

# 5

## (B)E(COM)ING

So how can you become a more cognizant communicator? Acknowledge your strong points, admit your growth areas, and take action toward the necessary adjustments by applying the Word Equity™ Model when approaching communication. Change does not have to be difficult, but it can feel foreign. Often foreign bodies are met with resistance. Embracing the opportunity to patiently walk through self-examination stages will result in a more refined approach to communication with others. For this cause, I have established clear steps to assist you on your journey to becoming more vigilant over the words that you speak and how you present in conversation.

The actionable steps are as follows:
**Believe it**- *Confidently expect truthfulness & transparency in your conversation.*
**Commit to it**- *Allow your belief to be built to such a point that you readily see the best in others.*
**Own it**- *Be accountable for your own actions & words.*

**Manage it**- *Consistently pursue harmony through your exchanges.*

Proper execution of the Word Equity™ Model will foster a language-rich environment that captures the heart's true intentions through words.

# 6

# PURPOSEFUL PROCESS

Being mindful of word choice is an active decision. In choosing a more passive approach, we may miss out on opportunities to effectively communicate what ought to be shared in a given conversation. Employing the practice of being intentional, particularly with words expressed, is an exercise that requires repeated or regular refinement.

I often consider what impression I wish to leave with the listener. What takeaway do I wish to offer through what has been imparted or expressed? Did I do a good job of clearly and effectively making the points expressed? Did the exchange create a call to action, fortify confidence or instead challenge self-concept? What story will be retold on behalf of the listener following our interaction? What message will be replayed in the mind of the listener after our correspondence? What words will be etched on the heart of the recipient as a result of our exchange?

While these impressions may feel like much to consider through a single exchange, when we place value on the words that we say and the purpose that each utterance serves to convey, we can more readily communicate our intentions.

Applying the Word Equity™ framework is an on-purpose process. When applied effectively and with consistency, the benefits of the Word Equity™ Model, which is defined as the essence of intentional speech that adds value to others, will show up in the relationships you choose to nurture. The ideal Word Equity™ Model practitioner is willing to challenge the standard way of communicating by relying on a robust lexicon of distinctive words available to master the message they intend to communicate.

# HOW ARE YOUR **WORDS** BEING PERCEIVED?

*"Golden* Opportunity"

| D | I | O | R |
|---|---|---|---|
| **Delivery** | Intentionality | **Opportunity** | **Responsibility** |
| Do others experience your communication towards them in a manner that adds value? | Do others recognize their significance when you share your thoughts, beliefs, desires, or hopes? | Do others readily adapt to your communication style & is that a good thing? | Do others understand their role in your life simply by how they experience you as a person? |

Word Equity™ Model

## RICH REPERTOIRE

The *Golden* Rule

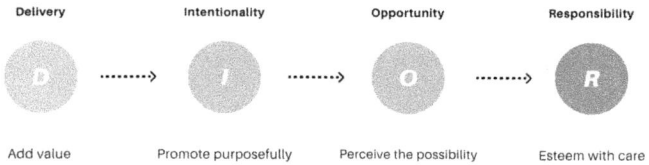

| Delivery | | Intentionality | | Opportunity | | Responsibility |
|----------|---|---------------|---|-------------|---|----------------|
| D | ·········> | I | ·········> | O | ·········> | R |
| Add value | | Promote purposefully | | Perceive the possibility | | Esteem with care |

Word Equity™ Model

# REFERENCES

*Merriam-Webster.com*. 2011. https://www.merriam-webster.com/dictionary. (19 April 2021)

www.ingramcontent.com/pod-product-compliance
Lightning Source LLC
Chambersburg PA
CBHW060045050426
42448CB00012B/3127